Ray's New Arithmetic Workbook

Series 1
Book Three

Rudolph Moore, Ph.D.
Betty Moore, M.A.

© **Mott Media, Inc., Publishers**
Milford, Michigan

Procedures for this Classic Curriculum Workbook:

Classic Curriculum is designed with the student in mind. It requires the use of other Classic Curriculum materials. Follow these steps:

Teacher:

1. *Remove* the test from the middle of the workbook.

2. *Read* Table of Contents and the "I can" statements at the top of the even numbered pages.

3. *Teach* the student the material or information on these pages. Until the student can read, the teacher must guide the student through each lesson.

4. *Read* the instructions to the student. Have the student tell you in his own words what he needs to do.

5. *Allow* the student to work independently as much as possible.

6. *Score* the work yourself, paying close attention to letter formation. (See picture key in Home Study Manual.)

7. *Ask* the student to rework wrong or careless work.

8. *Rescore* the reworked material.

9. *Praise* the student for his good effort, careful work, or other points that deserve praise.

10. *Review* and *Quiz* sections should be studied thoroughly.

11. *Give* each Quiz like a test. Review any items missed.

12. *Complete* the work lesson-by-lesson.

13. *Give* the final test (removed in step one) the day following completion of the last review.

14. *Score* the test and review any areas missed. The final score should be 80% or higher before advancing to the next workbook.

ISBN 0-88062-234-2

Table of Contents

Write Number Words
1 one   2 two

I can write the number words one and two.

Write the word for 1.*

one   one   one   one   one

one

Write the word for 2.

two   two   two   two   two

two

Write the words for 1 and 2.

one two   one two   one two

* Write over the screened letters. Practice writing the number words. Stress correct forming of letters and correct spelling of words.

2 (two)

Write the numbers in words.

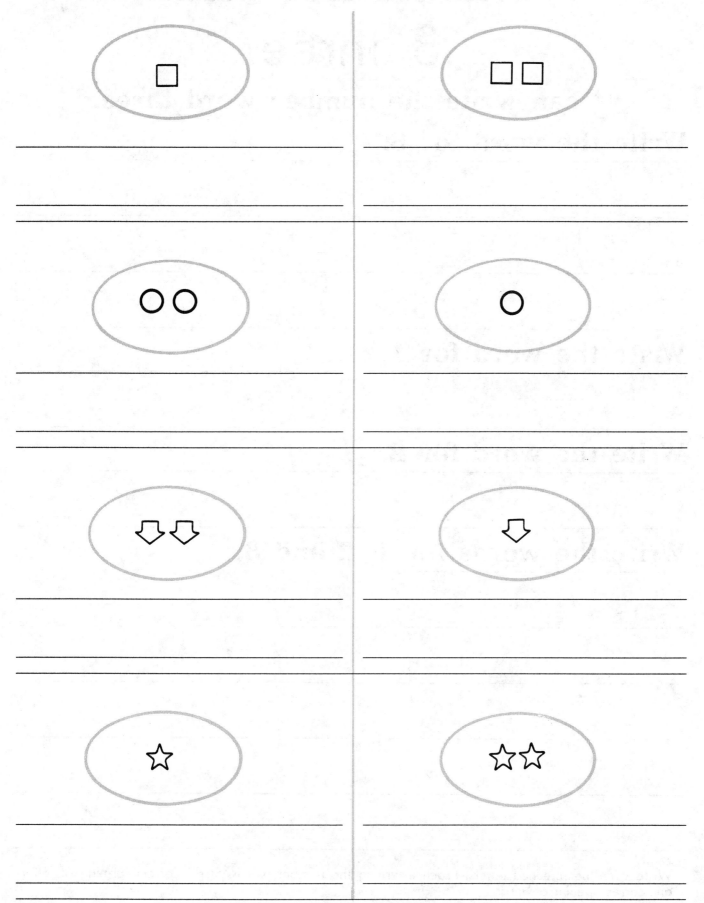

Write Number Words
3 three

Write the word for 3.*

three   three   three   three
three

Write the word for 1.

one

Write the word for 2.

two

Write the words for 1, 2 and 3.

one two three one two three

---

* Write over the screened letters. Practice writing the number words. Stress correct forming of letters and correct spelling of words.

Write the numbers in words.

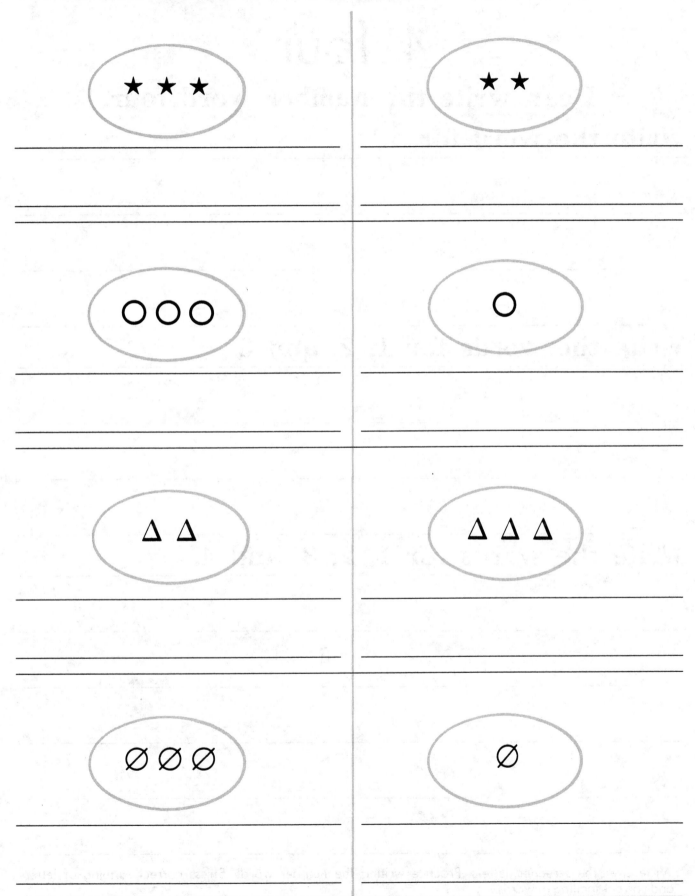

Write Number Words
4 four

I can write the number word four.

Write the word for 4.*

four four four four four
four

Write the words for 1, 2, and 3.

one two three   one two three

Write the words for 1, 2, 3, and 4.

one   two   three   four

* Write over the screened letters. Practice writing the number words. Stress correct forming of letters and correct spelling of words.

Write the numbers in words.

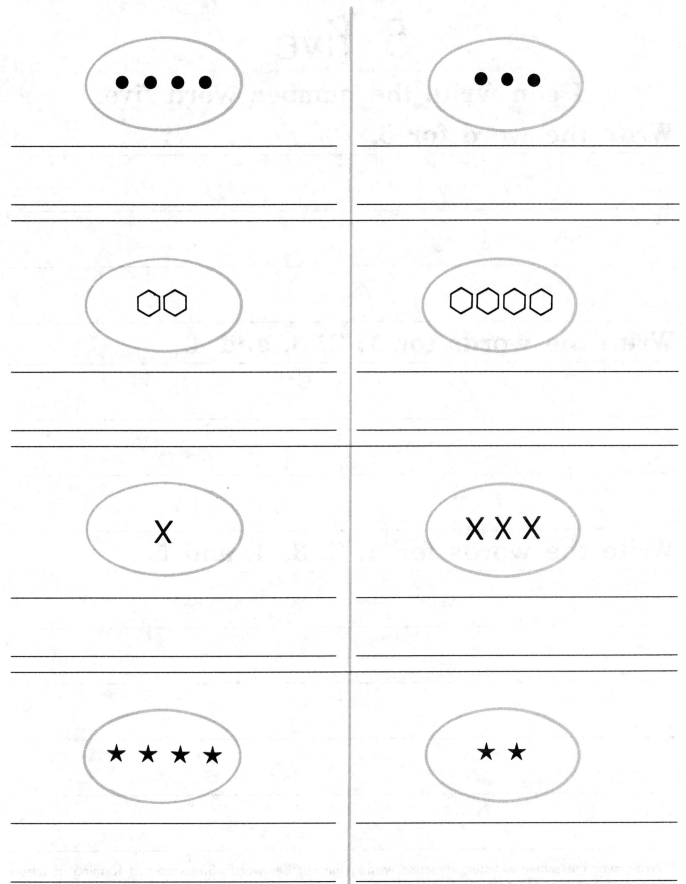

Write Number Words
5 five

I can write the number word five.

Write the word for 5.*

five   five   five   five   five

five

Write the words for 1, 2, 3, and 4.

one   two   three   four

Write the words for 1, 2, 3, 4, and 5.

one   two   three   four   five

* Write over the screened letters. Practice writing the number words. Stress correct forming of letters and correct spelling of words.

Write the numbers in words.

_____

_____

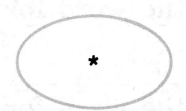

_____

_____

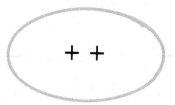

_____

_____

+ + + + +

_____

_____

_____

_____

☆ ☆ ☆

_____

_____

# # # # #

_____

_____

_____

_____

Quiz 1

Write the word for 1.*

one
_____

Write the word for 2.

two
_____

Write the word for 3.

three
_____

Write the word for 4.

four
_____

Write the word for 5.

five
_____

Write the number words for 1, 2, 3, 4, and 5.

_____

_____

_____

_____

* Write a row of each number word. Write 5 rows of one through five. Grade for accuracy of letter formation and correct spelling. Each line on top half of page 10, 6 points. Each line on bottom half of page 10, 8 points. Each counting activity, 5 points.

Write the numbers in words.

_____

_____

_____

_____

_____

_____

_____

_____

_____

_____

_____

_____

Write Number Words
6 six

I can write the number word six.

Write the word for 6.*

six   six   six   six   six

six

Write the words for 1, 2, 3, 4, and 5.

one   two   three   four   five

Write the words for 1, 2, 3, 4, 5, and 6.

one   two   three   four   five   six

* Write over the screened letters. Practice writing the number words. Stress correct forming of letters and correct spelling of words.

Write the numbers in words.

_____

_____

_____

_____

_____

_____

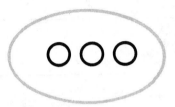

_____

_____

_____

_____

_____

_____

_____

_____

_____

_____

_____

_____

_____

_____

_____

_____

_____

_____

Write Number Words
7 seven

I can write the number word seven.

Write the word for 7.*

seven   seven   seven   seven

seven

Write the words for 1 through 6.

Write the words for 1 through 7.

one   two   three   four

five   six   seven

* Write over the screened letters. Practice writing the number words. Stress correct forming of letters and correct spelling of words.

Write the numbers in words.

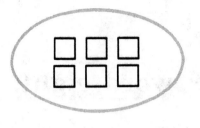 

_____

_____

_____

_____

_____

_____

_____

_____

Write Number Words
8 eight

I can write the number word eight.

Write the word for 8.*

eight   eight   eight   eight

eight

Write the words for 1 through 7.

one   two   three   four

five   six   seven

Write the words for 1 through 8.

one   two   three   four

five   six   seven   eight

* Write over the screened letters. Practice writing the number words. Stress correct forming of letters and correct spelling of words.

Write the numbers in words.

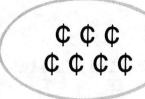

_____

_____

_____

_____

_____

_____

_____

_____

_____

_____

_____

_____

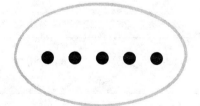

_____

_____

_____

_____

Write Number Words
9 nine

I can write the number word nine.

Write the word for 9.*

nine   nine   nine   nine

nine

Write the words for 1 through 8.

one   two   three   four

five   six   seven   eight

Write the words for 1 through 9.

one   two   three   four   five

six   seven   eight   nine

* Write over the screened letters. Practice writing the number words. Stress correct forming of letters and correct spelling of words.

Write the numbers in words.

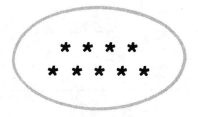

_____

_____

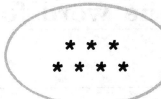

_____

_____

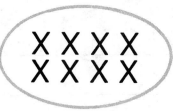

_____

_____

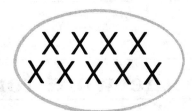

_____

_____

_____

_____

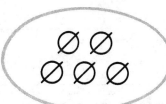

_____

_____

Quiz 2

Write the word for 6.[*]

six

Write the word for 7.

seven

Write the word for 8.

eight

Write the word for 9.

nine

Write the words for 1 through 5.

one   two   three   four   five

Write the number words for 1 through 9.

[*] Write a row of each number or numbers. Write words for one through nine 5 times. Use your own paper. Grade for accuracy of letter formation and correct spelling. Each line on page 20, 6 points. Each set of 1 through 9, 8 points. Each counting activity, 5 points.

20 (twenty)

Write the numbers in words.

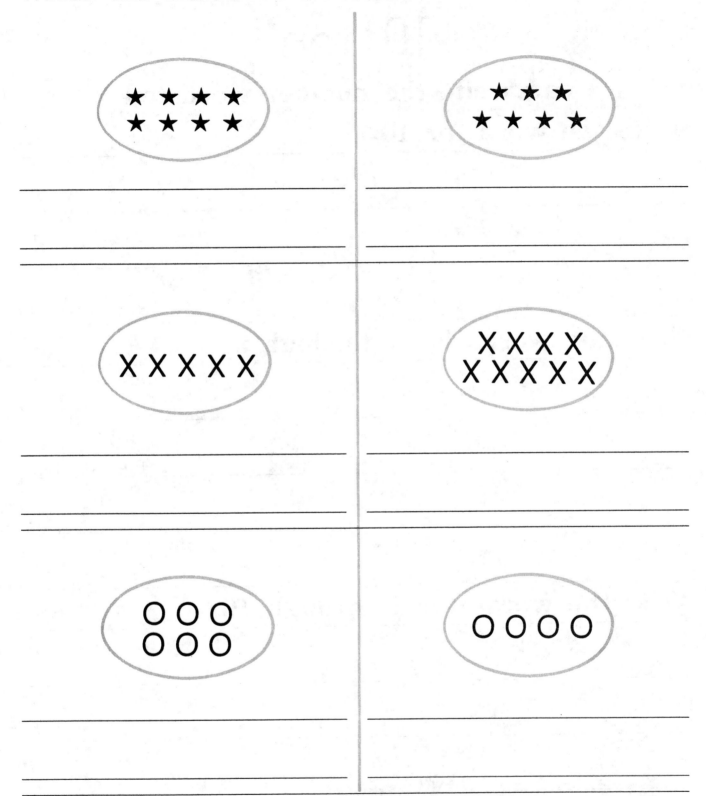

_____

_____

_____

_____

_____

_____

_____

_____

_____

_____

_____

_____

Write Number Words
10 ten

I can write the number word ten.

Write the word for 10.*

ten   ten   ten   ten   ten

ten

Write the words for 1 through 9.

one   two   three   four   five

six   seven   eight   nine

Write the words for 1 through 10.

one   two   three   four   five

six   seven   eight   nine   ten

* Write over the screened letters. Practice writing the number words. Stress correct forming of letters and correct spelling of words.

Write the numbers in words.

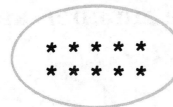

* * * * *
* * * * *

* * *

_____

_____

# # # # #

# # # #
# # # # #

_____

_____

+ + + +
+ + + +

+ + + + +
+ + + + +

_____

_____

¢ ¢ ¢ ¢ ¢
¢ ¢ ¢ ¢ ¢

¢ ¢ ¢
¢ ¢ ¢ ¢

_____

_____

Count and Write

I can count and write the number as a symbol and a word.

1	2	3	4	5
one	two	three	four	five

Write both the symbol and the word.

_____

_____

_____

_____

_____

_____

_____

_____

_____

_____

_____

_____

□ □ □ □

□

○ ○ ○

○ ○
○ ○ ○

¢

¢ ¢ ¢

Δ Δ Δ Δ

Δ Δ

Count and Write

I can count and write the number as a symbol and a word.

6	7	8	9	10
six	seven	eight	nine	ten

Write both the symbol and the word.

_____

_____

_____

_____

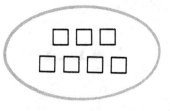

_____

_____

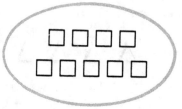

_____

_____

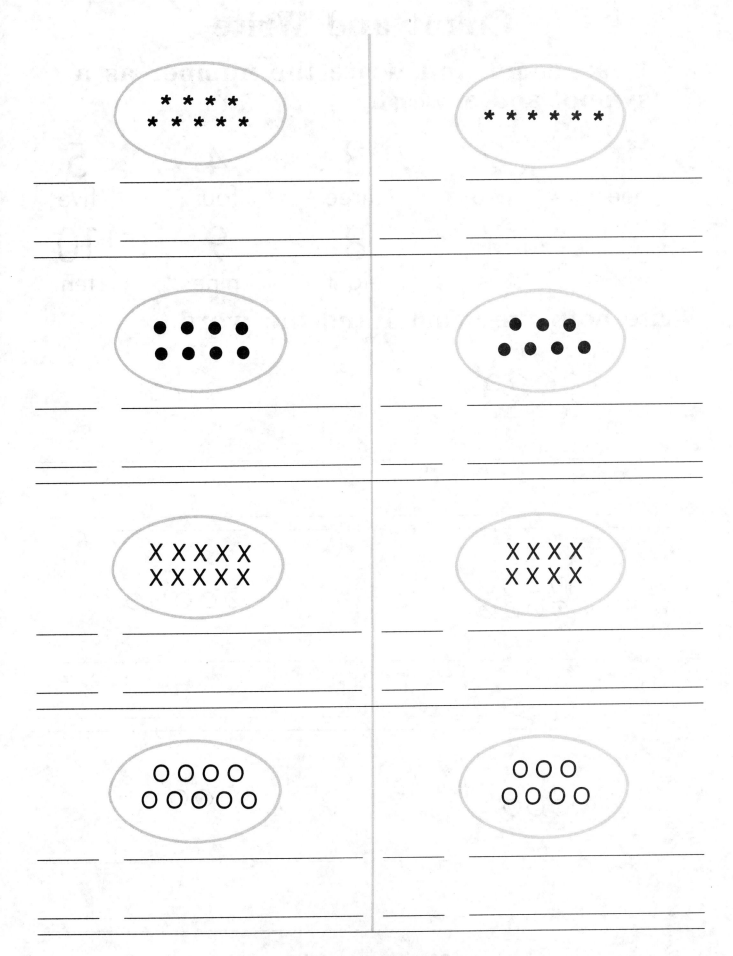

Count and Write

I can count and write the number as a symbol and a word.

1   one   2   two   3   three   4   four   5   five

6   six   7   seven   8   eight   9   nine   10   ten

Write both the symbol and the word.

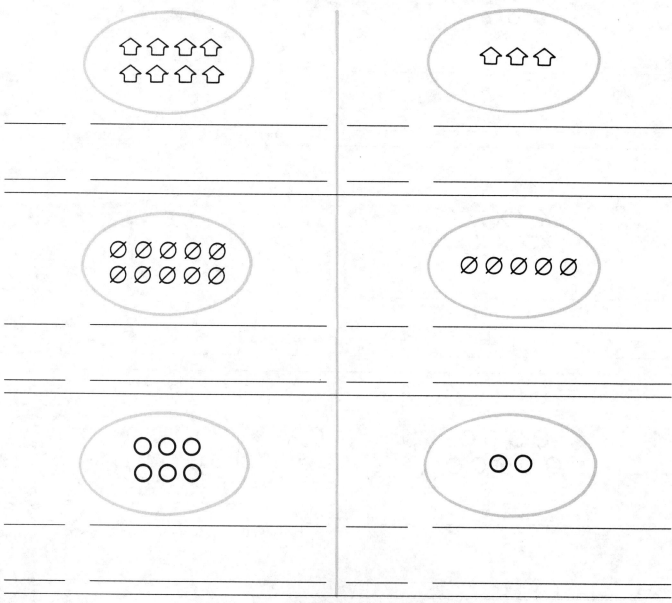

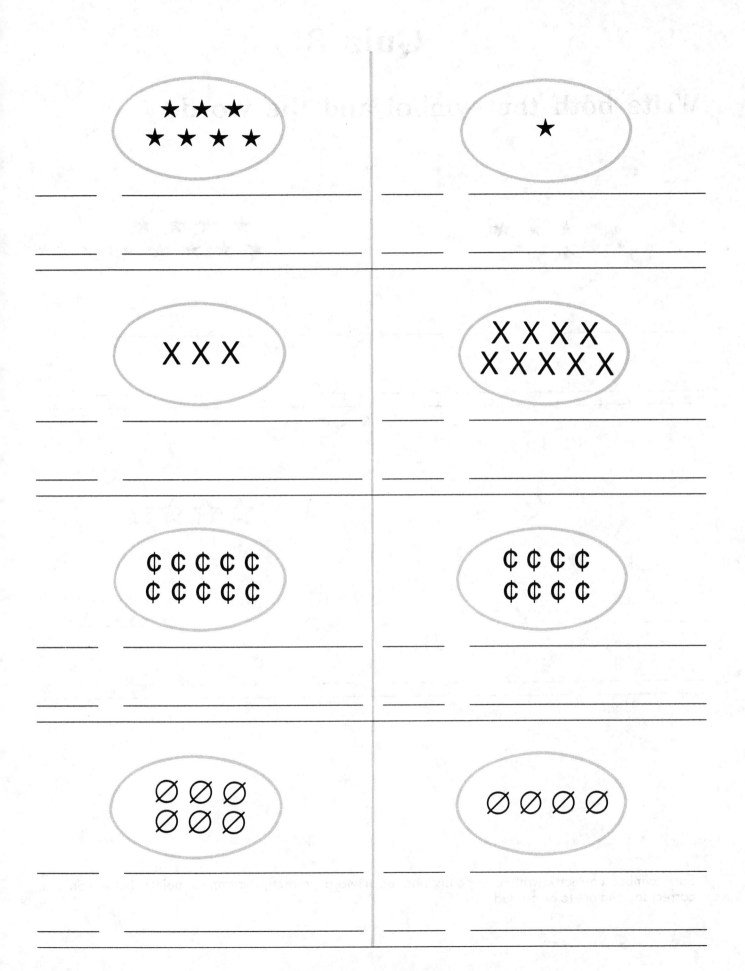

Quiz 3

Write both the symbol and the word.*

_____

_____

_____

_____

* Each symbol correctly written, 4 points and each word correctly written, 6 points. Formation and correct spelling are to be graded.

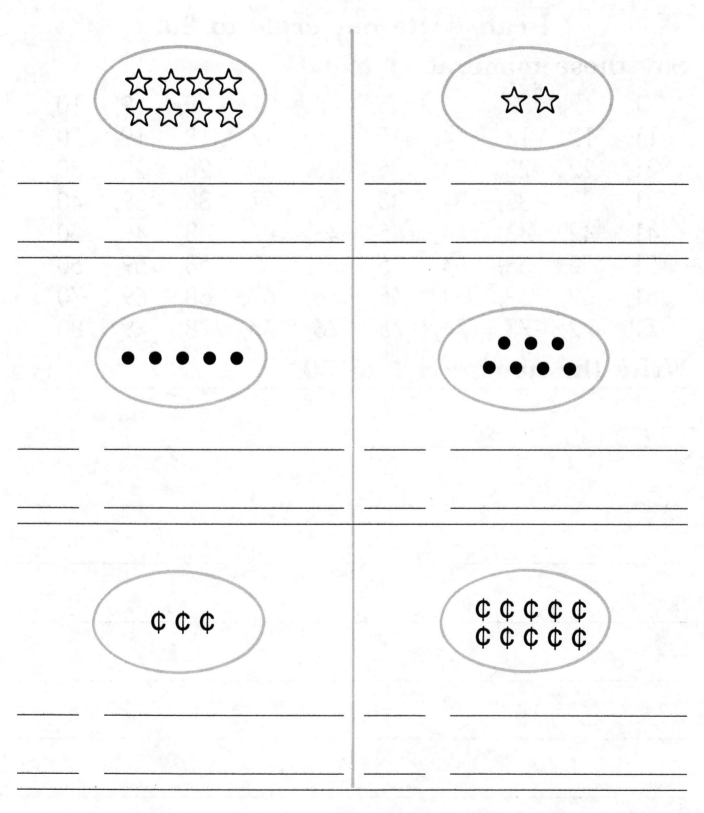

Write Numerals

I can write numerals to 80.

Say these numerals 1 to 80.

1,   2,   3,   4,   5,   6,   7,   8,   9, 10,
11, 12, 13, 14, 15, 16, 17, 18, 19, 20,
21, 22, 23, 24, 25, 26, 27, 28, 29, 30,
31, 32, 33, 34, 35, 36, 37, 38, 39, 40,
41, 42, 43, 44, 45, 46, 47, 48, 49, 50,
51, 52, 53, 54, 55, 56, 57, 58, 59, 60,
61, 62, 63, 64, 65, 66, 67, 68, 69, 70,
71, 72, 73, 74, 75, 76, 77, 78, 79, 80

Write the numerals 1 to 80.*

_____

_____

_____

_____

_____

_____

_____

* Teacher/tutor check for correct formation, correct spacing, and correct order.

Write the numerals 1 to 80.

_____

_____

_____

_____

_____

_____

_____

Draw dot-to-dot 60-80.

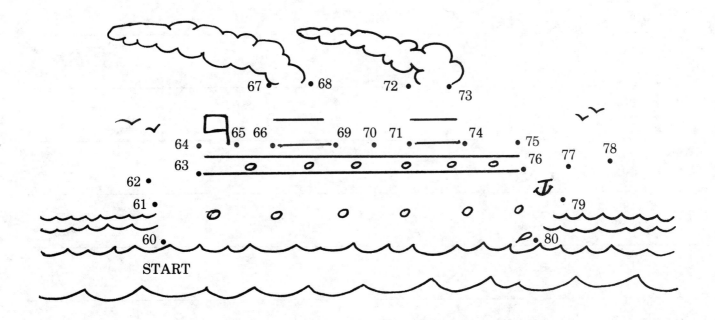

67 • • 68   72 • • 73

64 • • 65 66 • 69 70 71 • 74 • 75
                                    77   78
63 • o o o o o o • 76 •

62 •

61 •   • 79

60 • o o o o o o • 80

START

33 (thirty-three)

Write Numerals

I can write numerals to 90.

Say these numerals 1 to 90.

1,	2,	3,	4,	5,	6,	7,	8,	9,	10,
11,	12,	13,	14,	15,	16,	17,	18,	19,	20,
21,	22,	23,	24,	25,	26,	27,	28,	29,	30,
31,	32,	33,	34,	35,	36,	37,	38,	39,	40,
41,	42,	43,	44,	45,	46,	47,	48,	49,	50,
51,	52,	53,	54,	55,	56,	57,	58,	59,	60,
61,	62,	63,	64,	65,	66,	67,	68,	69,	70,
71,	72,	73,	74,	75,	76,	77,	78,	79,	80,
81,	82,	83,	84,	85,	86,	87,	88,	89,	90

Write the numerals 1 to 90.*

_____

_____

_____

_____

_____

_____

_____

_____

_____

* Teacher/tutor check for correct formation, correct spacing, and correct order.

34 (thirty-four)

Write the numerals 1 to 90.

_____

_____

_____

_____

_____

_____

_____

_____

_____

Draw dot-to-dot 65-90.

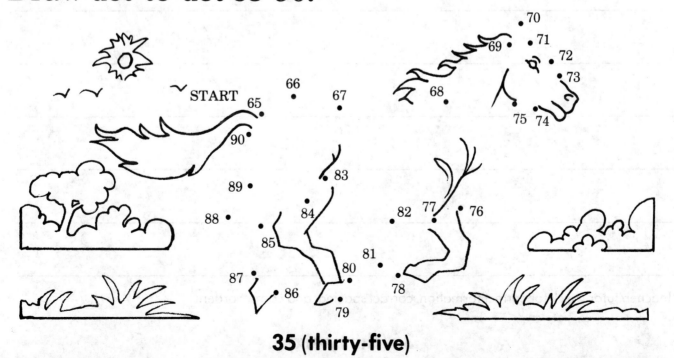

35 (thirty-five)

Write Numerals

I can write numerals to 100.

Say these numerals 1 to 100.

1,	2,	3,	4,	5,	6,	7,	8,	9,	10,
11,	12,	13,	14,	15,	16,	17,	18,	19,	20,
21,	22,	23,	24,	25,	26,	27,	28,	29,	30,
31,	32,	33,	34,	35,	36,	37,	38,	39,	40,
41,	42,	43,	44,	45,	46,	47,	48,	49,	50,
51,	52,	53,	54,	55,	56,	57,	58,	59,	60,
61,	62,	63,	64,	65,	66,	67,	68,	69,	70,
71,	72,	73,	74,	75,	76,	77,	78,	79,	80,
81,	82,	83,	84,	85,	86,	87,	88,	89,	90,
91,	92,	93,	94,	95,	96,	97,	98,	99,	100

Write the numerals 1 to 100.*

_____

_____

_____

_____

_____

_____

_____

_____

_____

* Teacher/tutor check for correct formation, correct spacing, and correct order.

Write the numerals 1 to 100.

_____

_____

_____

_____

_____

_____

_____

_____

_____

_____

Draw dot-to-dot 80-100.

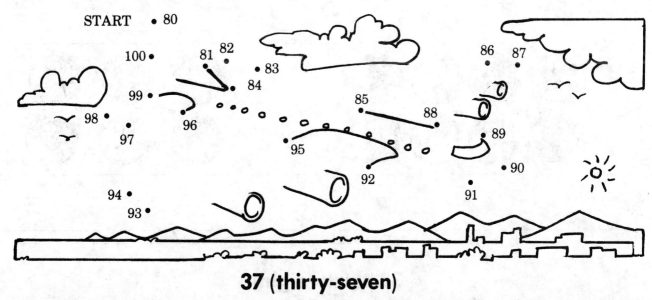

Symbols and Words

I can say numbers in symbols and words.

Draw a line to match the number symbol and number word.

1	five
2	three
3	one
4	four
5	six
6	two
7	ten
8	eight
9	seven
10	nine

Write the symbol and the word.

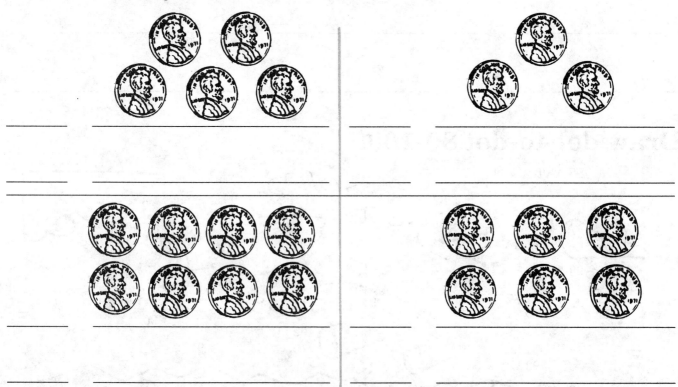

Draw a line to match the number of pennies to the number word.

four

five

three

two

one

Draw a line to match the number of pennies to the number word.

6 pennies	one penny
8 pennies	three pennies
4 pennies	six pennies
1 penny	five pennies
10 pennies	seven pennies
3 pennies	four pennies
5 pennies	eight pennies
9 pennies	two pennies
2 pennies	ten pennies
7 pennies	nine pennies

Quiz 4

Draw a line to match the number symbol and number word.

1	five
2	seven
3	two
4	six
5	three
6	one
7	ten
8	four
9	eight
10	nine

Write the number words for 1 through 10.

_____

_____

_____

_____

_____

* Each activity on page 40, 3 points each. Writing numerals 1 to 100, each row of ten numerals, 4 points. Check for correct order, formation, and spacing.

Write the numerals 1 to 100.

More Than or Less Than

Draw a ring around all numbers more than 62.

73	80	57	46	25
43	35	65	59	78

Draw a ring around all numbers less than 62.

63	48	68	70	28
52	79	17	30	80

Write more **or** less.

72 is _____ than 27.   58 is _____ than 28.

43 is _____ than 45.   15 is _____ than 25.

52 is _____ than 58.   22 is _____ than 44.

60 is _____ than 40.   33 is _____ than 11.

63 is _____ than 73.   55 is _____ than 60.

Draw a ring around the number that is more.

66 46	53 63
58 18	37 17
40 35	75 57

Draw a ring around the number that is less.

44 24	56 65
30 45	72 62
78 72	51 50

More Than or Less Than

Draw a ring around all numbers more than 65.

75	85	88	59	75
41	30	90	32	83

Draw a ring around all numbers less than 65.

69	46	78	60	48
57	80	15	20	72

Write more **or** less.

58 is _____ than 60.   80 is _____ than 70.

73 is _____ than 51.   61 is _____ than 69.

66 is _____ than 33.   89 is _____ than 85.

18 is _____ than 28.   73 is _____ than 78.

62 is _____ than 26.   90 is _____ than 50.

Ray's New Arithmetic Workbook

Series 1
Book Three Test

Name _____

Date _____

Possible score _____100_____

My score _____

Book Three Test

Write the numerals to 100 (40 points).

_____

_____

_____

_____

_____

_____

_____

_____

_____

Count and write the number words (16 points).

☐ ☐ ☐ ☐   ✸ ✸ ✸ ✸ ✸

_____   _____

_____   _____

∇ ∇ ∇ ∇ ∇ ∇ ∇ ∇   ○ ○ ○

_____   _____

_____   _____

Draw the objects and write the number (8 points).

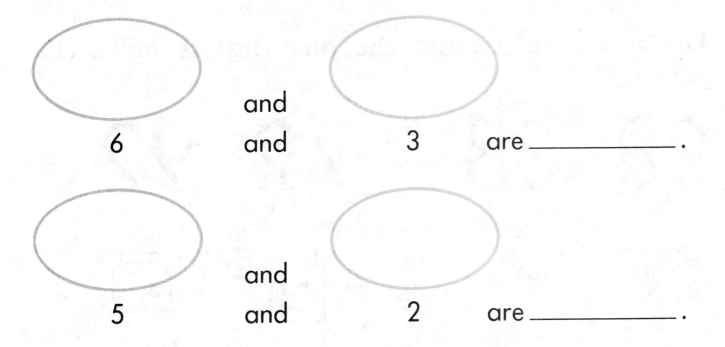

⬭   and   ⬭
6   and   3   are _____.

⬭   and   ⬭
5   and   2   are _____.

Read the story and write the number (20 points).

Ned saw six cows.   6 and 5 are _____ .
I saw five cows.

Ned and I saw _____ cows.

Seven days and six days are _____ days.

Five cats and eight cats are _____ cats.

Eight dogs and seven dogs are _____ dogs.

Nine nags and eight nags are _____ nags.

Draw a ring around the one that is more (16 points).

83 38 | 72 92

Draw a ring around the number that is more.

83 38	42 38
78 72	51 57
66 69	90 80

Draw a ring around the number that is less.

56 49	80 90
88 78	73 76
36 63	69 63

More Than or Less Than

I can say which number is more or less.

Draw a ring around all numbers more than 73.

92	28	65	98	24
58	88	79	33	82

Draw a ring around all numbers less than 73.

58	46	93	70	83
85	76	68	89	51

Write more **or** less.

90 is _____ than 60.   67 is _____ than 70.

73 is _____ than 79.   93 is _____ than 82.

49 is _____ than 45.   76 is _____ than 46.

64 is _____ than 68.   38 is _____ than 58.

80 is _____ than 90.   83 is _____ than 38.

Draw a ring around the number that is more.

96 98	62 57
75 85	38 83
83 81	73 75

Draw a ring around the number that is less.

92 96	47 74
89 79	98 89
38 48	67 76

More Than or Less Than

I can show the one that is more or less.

Draw a line to match the ones that are the same

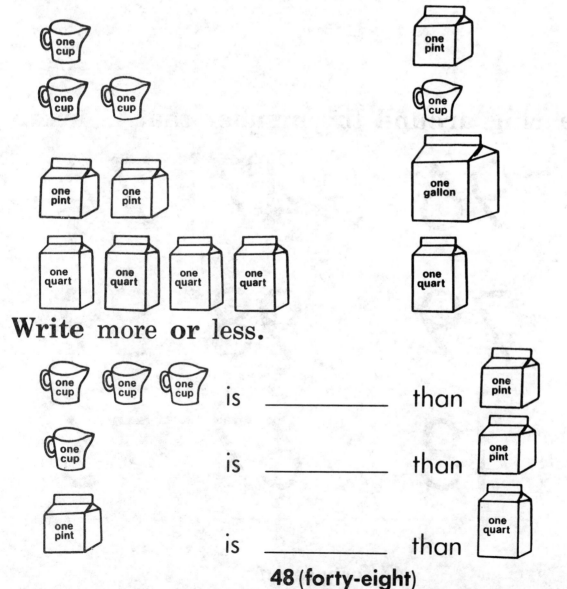

Write more or less.

_____ cup _____ cup _____ cup   is _____ than   one pint

one cup   is _____ than   one pint

one pint   is _____ than   one quart

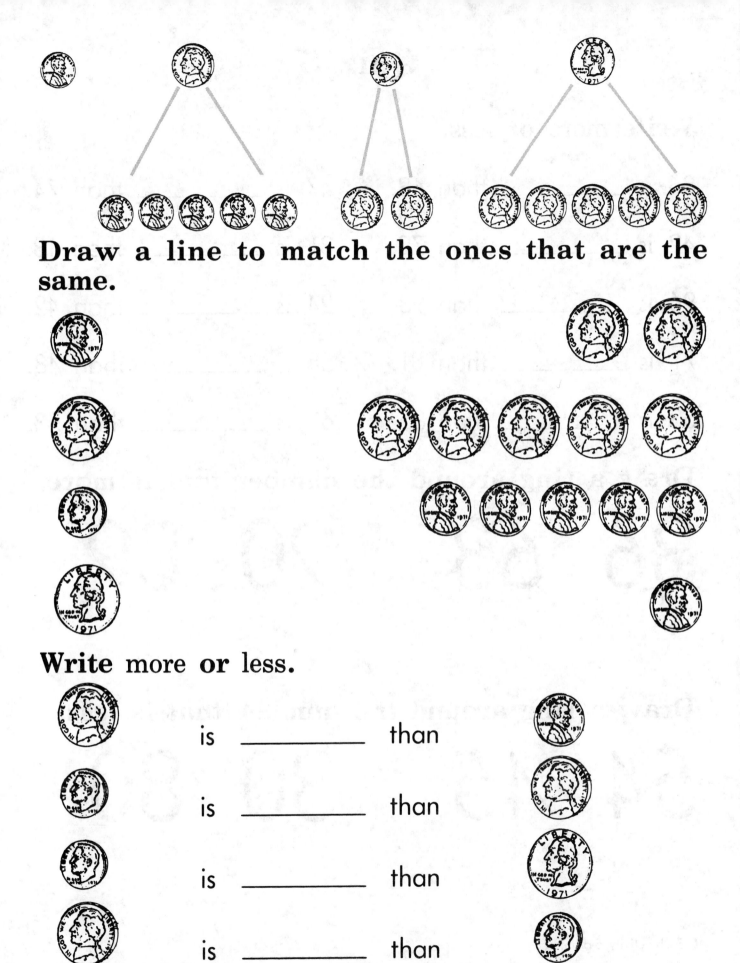

Draw a line to match the ones that are the same.

Write more **or** less.

is _____ than

is _____ than

is _____ than

is _____ than

Quiz 5

Write more or less.*

86 is _____ than 68.   47 is _____ than 74.

42 is _____ than 72.   31 is _____ than 13.

96 is _____ than 93.   24 is _____ than 42.

71 is _____ than 81.   58 is _____ than 48.

53 is _____ than 35.   63 is _____ than 73.

Draw a ring around the number that is more.

36 63   90 89

Draw a ring around the number that is less.

54 45   30 80

* Each activity, 5 points.

Write more or less.

is _____ than

is _____ than

is _____ than

is _____ than

is _____ than

is _____ than

Perfect score   100

My score   _____

Combine Sets

I can draw the objects and write the number.

Draw the objects and write the number.*

(⬭)

and

1   and   1   are _____.

and

1   and   2   are _____.

and

2   and   2   are _____.

and

2   and   3   are _____.

and

3   and   1   are _____.

* The student is to draw the number of objects indicated in each oval. Then have the student count the objects and write the answer.

Draw a line to match the ones that are the same.[*]

1 and 2   3 and 2

2 and 3   2 and 1

4 and 1   3 and 1

1 and 3   1 and 4

Draw a line to match the ones that are the same.[*]

1 and 3   1 and 2

2 and 1   4 and 1

2 and 3   2 and 2

[*] Use counters.

Stories

I can read stories and write the number.

Read the story and write the number.*

I see one cow.
Tom sees two cows.

1 and 2 are_____

Tom and I see _____ cows.

Ned saw two red hens.
Tom sees two brown hens.

2 and 2 are_____

Ned and Tom saw _____ hens.

Ann had one new cap.
I had three new caps.

1 and 3 are_____

Ann and I had _____new caps.

The dog has two pups.
The cat has three kits.

2 and 3 are_____

The dog and cat have _____ pups and kits.

* The student should first read the story. The student may then draw pictures of the story or use counters to demonstrate the story. Finally the student counts the objects and writes the number on both lines.

Read the story and write the number.*

One pig and one pig are _____ pigs.

Two kids and one kid are _____ kids.

Two cats and two cats are _____ cats.

Three apes and two apes are _____ apes.

Four rats and one rat are _____ rats.

Three hens and one hen are _____ hens.

One dog and two dogs are _____ dogs.

Two bats and three bats are _____ bats.

One nag and three nags are _____ nags.

One top and four tops are _____ tops.

* Use counters.

Combine Sets

I can draw the objects and write the number.

Draw the objects and write the number.*

⬭   and
3   and   3   are _____.

⬭
             and
2   and   4   are _____.

⬭
             and
3   and   4   are _____.

⬭
             and
5   and   1   are _____.

⬭
             and
2   and   5   are _____.

* The student is to draw the number of objects indicated in each oval. Then have the student count the objects and write the answer.

Draw a line to match the ones that are the same.*

3 and 4   4 and 2

5 and 1   5 and 2

2 and 4   4 and 3

2 and 5   1 and 6

6 and 1   1 and 5

Draw a line to match the ones that are the same.*

3 and 3   4 and 1

4 and 3   2 and 4

2 and 3   3 and 1

2 and 2   2 and 5

* Use counters.

Stories

I can read stories and write the number.

Read the story and write the number.*

I see three red cows.   3 and 3 are_____
Ned sees three brown cows.

Ned and I see _____ cows.

Ann saw two apes at the zoo.   2 and 4 are_____
Tom saw four apes at the circus.

Ann and Tom saw _____ apes.

The man had five tops.   5 and 1 are_____
I had one red top.

The man and I had _____ tops.

He had six cows.   6 and 1 are_____
Tom had one cow.

He and Tom have _____ cows.

See two bats in the tree.   2 and 5 are_____
See five bats in the cave.

We can see _____ bats.

* The student should first read the story. The student may then draw pictures of the story or use counters to demonstrate the story. Finally the student counts the objects and writes the number on both lines.

Read the story and write the number.*

Two tops and five tops are _____ tops.

Three apes and four apes are _____ apes.

Six flies and one fly are _____ flies.

Two nags and four nags are _____ nags.

Five cows and one cow are _____ cows.

Two bats and three bats are _____ bats.

Three dogs and three dogs are _____ dogs.

Two pigs and two pigs are _____ pigs.

One hen and two hens are _____ hens.

Three kids and one kid are _____ kids.

* Use counters.

Quiz 6

Draw the objects and write the number.*

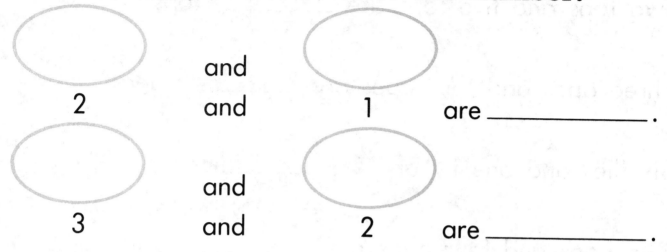

2   and
    and   1   are _____.

3   and
    and   2   are _____.

Draw a line to match the ones that are the same.*

1 and 3   4 and 1

3 and 2   2 and 4

3 and 3   4 and 3

2 and 5   2 and 2

* Each answer (total 20), 5 points each.

Read the story and write the number.

Ned sees one cow.   1 and 2 are_____
Tom sees two cows.

Ned and Tom see _____ cows.

I see three red tops.   3 and 4 are_____
Ann sees four red tops.

Ann and I see _____ red tops.

Five dogs and one dog are _____ dogs.

Three kits and three kits are _____ kits.

Two pigs and two pigs are _____ pigs.

Five tops and two tops are _____ tops.

One hen and two hens are _____ hens.

Two nags and four nags are _____ nags.

Perfect score   100

My score   _____

61 (sixty-one)

Combine Sets

I can draw the objects and write the number.

Draw the objects and write the number.*

and

4   and   4   are _____.

and

6   and   2   are _____.

and

5   and   3   are _____.

and

4   and   5   are _____.

and

6   and   3   are _____.

* The student is to draw the number of objects indicated in each oval. Then have the student count the objects and write the answer.

Draw a line to match the ones that are the same.*

2 and 7   5 and 3

4 and 4   4 and 1

2 and 5   6 and 3

4 and 2   4 and 3

2 and 3   3 and 3

Draw a line to match the ones that are the same.*

6 and 2   5 and 2

3 and 1   8 and 1

4 and 5   7 and 1

6 and 1   2 and 4

5 and 1   2 and 2

* Use counters.

Stories

I can read stories and write the number.

Read the story and write the number.*

I saw four dogs.   4 and 4 are_____ .
Ned saw four dogs.

Ned and I saw _____ dogs.

May saw three cats.   3 and 6 are_____ .
Ann saw six cats.

May and Ann saw _____ cats.

Tom saw eight rats.   8 and 1 are_____ .
The man saw one rat.

The man and Tom saw _____ rats.

There were seven kids in the   7 and 2 are_____ .
pen.
There were two kids in the yard.

Together there were _____ kids.

Ann is five years old.   5 and 4 are_____ .
Ned is four years old.

Five years and four years are _____ years.

* The student should first read the story. The student may then draw pictures of the story or use counters to demonstrate the story. Finally the student counts the objects and writes the number on both lines.

Read the story and write the number.*

Four pigs and five pigs are _____ pigs.

Seven cows and one cow are _____ cows.

Three kids and six kids are _____ kids.

Four hens and four hens are _____ hens.

Two apes and seven apes are _____ apes.

Eight rats and one rat are _____ rats.

Three cats and five cats are _____ cats.

Six elk and two elk are _____ elk.

Two dogs and three dogs are _____ dogs.

Three bats and three bats are _____ bats.

* Use counters.

Combine Sets

I can draw the objects and write the number.

Draw the objects and write the number.*

and

5   and   5   are _____ .

and

6   and   5   are _____ .

and

6   and   6   are _____ .

and

8   and   2   are _____ .

and

7   and   4   are _____ .

* The student is to draw the number of objects indicated in each oval. Then have the student count the objects and write the answer.

Draw a line to match the ones that are the same.*

5 and 3		5 and 7
6 and 2		2 and 8
7 and 3		3 and 5
7 and 5		3 and 7
8 and 2		4 and 6
9 and 3		2 and 6
6 and 4		3 and 9

Draw a line to match the ones that are the same.*

9 and 1		4 and 5
7 and 4		6 and 6
3 and 4		5 and 5
6 and 3		4 and 4
4 and 8		8 and 3
5 and 3		5 and 2

* Use counters.

Stories

I can read stories and write the number.

Read the story and write the number.*

I can see eight cows.   8 and 4 are_____.
Ned can see four cows.

Ned and I can see _____ cows.

Ann saw nine cats.   9 and 3 are_____.
Tom saw three cats.

Ann and Tom saw _____ cats.

See four bats in the tree.   4 and 7 are_____
See seven bats in the cave.

We can see _____ bats.

She had six caps.   6 and 6 are_____
The man had six caps.

She and the man had _____ caps.

May had two red dogs.   2 and 8 are_____
Ned had eight brown dogs.

May and Ned had _____ dogs.

* The student should first read the story. The student may then draw pictures of the story or use counters to demonstrate the story. Finally the student counts the objects and writes the number on both lines.

Read the story and write the number.*

Nine cows and three cows are _____ cows.

Six cats and four cats are _____ cats.

Five hens and five hens are _____ hens.

Three nags and eight nags are _____ nags.

Five caps and six caps are _____ caps.

Seven bats and five bats are _____ bats.

Four elk and eight elk are _____ elk.

Three pigs and seven pigs are _____ pigs.

Nine flies and one fly are _____ flies.

Two tops and nine tops are _____ tops.

* Use counters.

69 (sixty-nine)

Quiz 7

Draw the objects and write the number.*

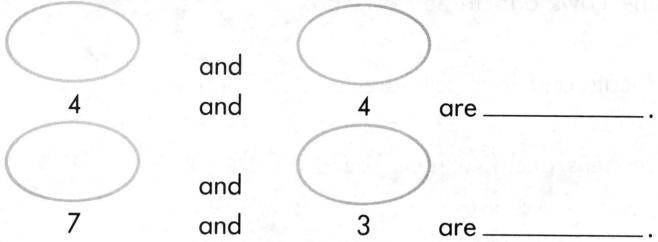

4   and
4   and
   4   are _____ .

7   and
7   and
   3   are _____ .

Draw a line to match the ones that are the same.*

5   and   5   7   and   4

9   and   3   2   and   7

4   and   5   6   and   4

3   and   8   5   and   7

* Each answer (total 20), 5 points each.

Read the story and write the number.

The man had six caps.   6 and 3 are _____
The boy had three caps.

The man and boy had _____ caps.

I saw eight apes at the zoo.   8 and 4 are _____
Ann saw four apes at the circus.

Ann and I saw _____ apes.

Seven hens and five hens are _____ hens.

Nine nags and three nags are _____ nags.

Three pigs and eight pigs are _____ pigs.

Six tops and three tops are _____ tops.

Five cats and six cats are _____ cats.

Eight dogs and two dogs are _____ dogs.

Perfect score   100

My score   _____

Combine Sets

I can draw the objects and write the number.

Draw the objects and write the number.*

5 and 8 and are _____ .

7 and 7 and are _____ .

7 and 6 and are _____ .

8 and 6 and are _____ .

7 and 8 and are _____ .

* The student is to draw the number of objects indicated in each oval. Then have the student count the objects and write the answer.

72 (seventy-two)

Draw a line to match the ones that are the same.*

9 and 4   2 and 9

8 and 6   4 and 9

9 and 6   4 and 8

8 and 4   5 and 6

9 and 2   6 and 9

6 and 5   6 and 8

Draw a line to match the ones that are the same.*

7 and 6   6 and 8

8 and 7   5 and 7

7 and 7   8 and 5

6 and 6   9 and 6

4 and 7   3 and 8

* Use counters.

73 (seventy-three)

Stories

I can read stories and write the number.

Read the story and write the number.*

There were six old apes at the zoo.
They will get six more.

6 and 6 are _____

Then the zoo will have _____ old apes.

We can spin four tops.
We will spin eight more tops.

4 and 8 are _____

We can spin _____ tops.

We saw three log huts.
Then we saw five more log huts.

3 and 5 are _____

We saw _____ log huts.

Mother had five tubs.
She got two more tubs.

5 and 2 are _____

Mother had _____ tubs.

Nine cows were in the field.
Four cows were in the pen.

9 and 4 are _____

Altogether there were _____ cows.

* The student should first read the story. The student may then draw pictures of the story or use counters to demonstrate the story. Finally the student counts the objects and writes the number on both lines.

Read the story and write the number.*

Eight hens and five hens are _____ hens.

Six dogs and seven dogs are _____ dogs.

Seven cats and eight cats are _____ cats.

Nine bats and five bats are _____ bats.

Six flies and nine flies are _____ flies.

Eight nags and six nags are _____ nags.

Five elk and nine elk are _____ elk.

Six tops and six tops are _____ tops.

Three cows and eight cows are _____ cows.

Seven caps and seven caps are _____ caps.

* Use counters.

Combine Sets

I can draw the objects and write the number.

Draw the objects and write the number.*

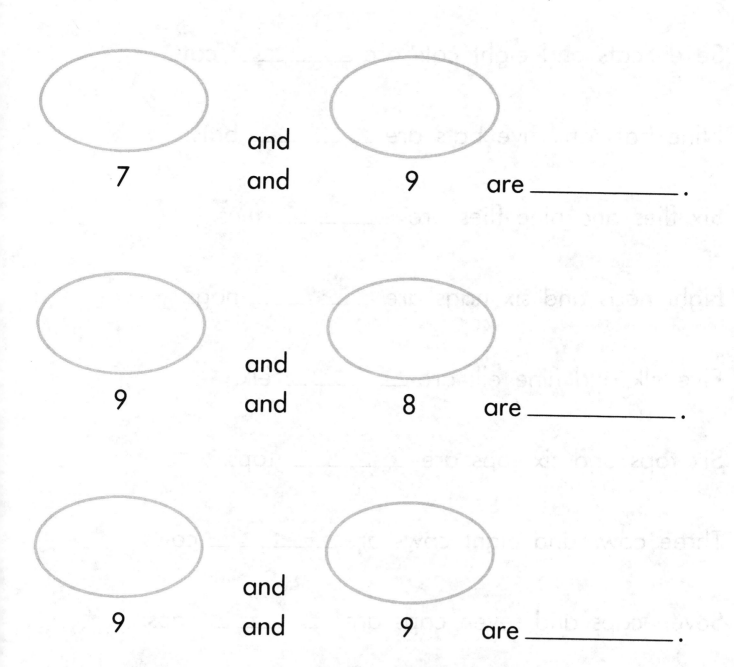

7 and and 9 are _____.

9 and and 8 are _____.

9 and and 9 are _____.

* The student is to draw the number of objects indicated in each oval. Then have the student count the objects and write the answer.

Draw a line to match the ones that are the same.[*]

9 and 7	6 and 8
8 and 9	4 and 9
9 and 6	9 and 8
7 and 8	6 and 9
8 and 6	7 and 9
9 and 4	8 and 7

Draw a line to match the ones that are the same.[*]

8 and 8	6 and 8
5 and 5	7 and 6
6 and 6	9 and 7
7 and 7	6 and 4
9 and 4	9 and 3

* Use counters.

Stories

I can read stories and write the number.

Read the story and write the number.[*]

Mother had nine pins.   9 and 6 are_____.
She got six more pins.

Now Mother has _____ pins.

One cat had four kits.   4 and 7 are_____.
This cat had seven kits.

Both cats had _____ kits.

I saw seven jays.   7 and 8 are_____.
Ned saw eight jays.

Ned and I saw _____ jays.

Ann had nine toys.   9 and 5 are_____.
Tom had five toys.

Ann and Tom had _____ toys.

May had seven fans.   7 and 6 are_____.
Ann had six fans.

May and Ann had _____ fans.

[*] The student should first read the story. The student may then draw pictures of the story or use counters to demonstrate the story. Finally the student counts the objects and writes the number on both lines.

Read the story and write the number.*

Nine fans and seven fans are _____ fans.

Eight beds and nine beds are _____ beds.

Nine tops and nine tops are _____ tops.

Six cats and nine cats are _____ cats.

Eight dogs and eight dogs are _____ dogs.

Six bats and eight bats are _____ bats.

Seven pigs and seven pigs are _____ pigs.

Nine flies and five flies are _____ flies.

Eight caps and six caps are _____ caps.

Seven days and five days are _____ days.

* Use counters.

Quiz 8

Draw the objects and write the number.*

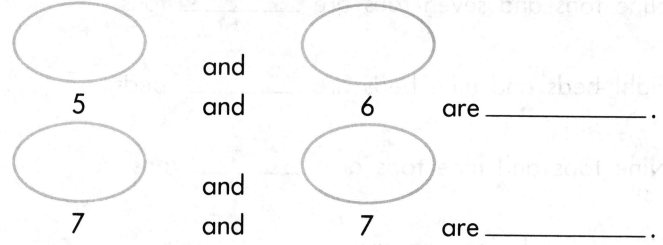

5   and   6   are _____.

7   and   7   are _____.

Draw a line to match the ones that are the same.*

7 and 9   9 and 6

7 and 8   8 and 8

8 and 9   5 and 9

7 and 7   9 and 8

* Each answer (total 20), 5 points each.

80 (eighty)

Read the story and write the number.

May had six fans.   6 and 9 are_____.
Ann had nine fans.

May and Ann had _____ fans.

The man had seven red dogs.   7 and 8 are_____
Ned had eight brown dogs.

The man and Ned had _____ dogs.

Nine days and nine days are _____ days.

Seven rats and nine rats are _____ rats.

Eight cats and five cats are _____ cats.

Nine nags and eight nags are _____ nags.

Eight pigs and seven pigs are _____ pigs.

Seven dogs and nine dogs are _____ dogs.

Perfect score   100

My score   _____

81 (eighty-one)

Write Number Words

Write the number words for 1 through 10.

one

two

three

four

five

six

seven

eight

nine

ten

Write the numbers in words.

☆ ☆ ☆ ☆ ☆ ☆   ⬡ ⬡ ⬡ ⬡

_____ _____

_____ _____

☐ ☐ ☐ ☐ ☐ ☐ ☐ ☐   △ △ △ △ △
             △ △ △ △ △

_____ _____

_____ _____

○ ○ ○ ○ ○   ⬠ ⬠ ⬠ ⬠ ⬠ ⬠ ⬠

_____ _____

_____ _____

★ ★ ★ ★ ★ ★ ★ ★ ★ ★ ○ ○ ○ ○

_____ _____

_____ _____

83 (eighty-three)

Write Numerals

Write the numerals to 100.

Write the numerals 1 to 100.

More Than or Less Than

Draw a ring around all numbers more than 50.

65	46	35	87	16
72	93	28	53	76

Draw a ring around all numbers less than 50.

43	54	86	38	41
72	98	68	25	14

Write more **or** less.

67 is _____ than 76.   19 is _____ than 91.

28 is _____ than 82.   31 is _____ than 13.

96 is _____ than 69.   53 is _____ than 35.

45 is _____ than 54.   87 is _____ than 78.

75 is _____ than 57.   38 is _____ than 83.

Draw a ring around the one that is more.

67   69   96   91

33   44   73   78

Draw a ring around the one that is less.

42   24   22   44

39   93   58   48

Combined Sets

I can draw the objects and write the
number.

Draw the objects and write the number.*

◯   and
                    ◯
3   and   2   are _____ .

◯   ◯
         and
4   and   4   are _____ .

◯   ◯
         and
6   and   4   are _____ .

◯   ◯
         and
3   and   6   are _____ .

◯   ◯
         and
3   and   4   are _____ .

* The student is to draw the number of objects indicated in each oval. Then have the student count
the objects and write the answer.

Draw a line to match the ones that are the same.*

9 and 4	9 and 6
7 and 8	8 and 8
8 and 6	8 and 5
7 and 9	7 and 4
8 and 4	7 and 7
5 and 6	6 and 6

Read the story and write the number.*

Mother has seven pins.   7 and 9 are_____.
She got nine more pins.

Now Mother has _____ pins.

Eight dogs and eight dogs are _____ dogs.

Six bats and seven bats are _____ bats.

Nine flies and five flies are _____ flies.

* Use counters.